Early One Sunday Morning

By:

Domo Jones

Church *Announcements*

> What's the life of a PK? You see everything but say nothing. You know a lot but don't speak a thing.
>
> ~ Domo Jones

"First, Giving Honor to God"

So, when I sit back on everything that comes with the title of this book, I tend to ask myself, "why me?" The answer is simple. God chose me. The beautiful thing is that sometimes we forget that God created us KNOWING everything we'd face in life. I say that because, if the Creator created us, shouldn't he have already had things in place to help us when we hit those unfamiliar places?! Trust me, I didn't piece it together right away either! I must say, the Man is pretty dope having the answers to the questions He KNEW we would ask, but ain't even asked yet! And with all that comes with this life, it's definitely not for the faint at heart, but He knew one day I would use my story as a leeway to make His name known. My experiences made me stronger, tougher, accepting, nonjudgmental, and most of all...loving. Y'all know I'll tell you I love you in a quick minute lol I don't care if it's a stranger, oh, you gone get this love! And you better say it back shoot! Yes, my life means going toe-to-toe with the devil, but this is what I've prepared for! And clearly he doesn't know the warrior he's facing, but he gone learn real quick that I AIN'T THE ONE OR THE TWO YOU WANNA COME NEAR!

Seems like that's the end of it, huh? I know what I'm doing and how it all works, so I'm good. Well quite the contrary. You see, all those powerful punchlines you just read was no where near my mindset until I was going through life. Believe me, this me wasn't always what you see. It was a process that took some major growing. Heres what imma do, I'm going to take you on a lil reverse run. I need you to see how I am today FIRST and take you through what it took to get me here. I figured, being God created our end from our beginning, why can't I use that same method to share my story? Ahhh got you thinking! Y'all know I'm atypical, I always have to add my lil twist to things lol It'll be interesting to see me today but know me back then too. So, you already know what to do: sit back, relax and go on this journey with me because without further or do I present to you...the rest of this book lol Yeah I couldn't think of anything more grand than that! Anyway, go on now, as you were...

"Something on the inside, working on the outside..." or how bout this, "Living He loved me, dying He saved me.." Uh oh, I done started something now!! I see some hands clapping and toes tapping lol That got your attention huh?! So, those were the songs I heard growing up. If you grew up in church then need I say more?! Cuz you already know we can stay there all day! That same beat can go with at least 200 songs!! Has anyone else noticed that except me?!

Man!! I mean, just be going for hours with that same dawg on tempo lol Lowkey tho, old school toe tappers were some of the greatest songs ever written! It's the lyrics for me! But for those who have not a clue as to what in the world I'm talking about, there's a seat open just for you! Make sure you get all you can to absorb the things you're about to hear, cuz I'll tell you now, being I was raised in church, after this you will be too, trust lol Oh, and for those "used too's", you're STILL a church kid! If Grandma was a Missionary or Grandpa was the head Deacon and they made you go to Sunday School, YOU'RE A CHURCH KID!! I don't even know why you thought different?! No, no, no beloved, whether you'd stop going or still do today, those memories will forever be embedded in you precious. And YOU know that! I guess you can say we're ALL just a big group of church kids! And if you don't know, now yuh know! Gloray, Glooooray!! (Did you start signing?! See!! I told you lol)

"You Can't Just Join In"

Let's address the elephant in the room, shall we? So yeah Dōmo, you grew up in church. Congratulations me too, what's the book about tho?! I'm glad you asked! (Even if you didn't, just act like you did, k?!) For those that know me, know I don't ever come simple. There's always some kind of "dun dun dun" plot twist in my life! My first book can definitely vouch for that lol You ready for it?! Ok here it is..both my dads are Pastors!! Dun dun dun!! See I told you I always have plot twists! And to twist the plot even tighter, they're Pastors in two total different denominations aka COGIC and Nondenominational! Whew, it's like a double whammy for you ain't it?! Now riddle me this: how many people do YOU know that's a PK twice?! I'm still waiting for someone to claim their prize! One? Of course. But two? Come on, now! Like, what?! Is this a joke that I'm only participating in, cuz what is really going here?! I know you've never heard of it, cuz I ain't never heard of describing my own self lol How is this even a "thing"?! Is this even legal in the state of California?! If so, let me gone head and pack, say my so long, farewell's and get the bless on!

I mean, do I even get an option to accept or deny?! No but foreal, the pressure of life that has come with this is beyond me!! Being one PK is a lot but we we already know that, so then you gone hit us with the double whammy, TWO?! Okay, flag on the play! Where do I draw the line?! Enough is enough! Bowed heads, so hear me out! Father God I know you know what you're doin and all, but uhh you sure about this one?! Some things only come out through fasting AND praying...

Let me just give you all a little insight of what the life of a PK...times two, is REALLY all about. Fasten your seatbelts, and so it begins...For the record, because some people get real confused...a PK is a Pastor's kid NOT Preachers kid. There is a huge difference, Amen. Don't be tryna put us under the same category because the requirements and Bi-laws are not the same! Aht, aht! You can't just join in, you have to be born in that thang! Now, where were we...I didn't grow up as a PK, but I definitely grew up in Church! I had a normal childhood like everyone else, oh but when it came time for Church, that's a whole different other other category that's not to be toyed with! It didn't matter what was going on, if we had to be at Church, no questions were asked because we were going. There was nothing else to discuss because Church was our final destination, Amen! I'll get to what it's like being in two denominations, but for now, I'm going to share the commonalities. Here we go...

My parents, Uncles, Grandparents, Great Grands, second Cousin on my dads side twice removed and the pets, were all over something in the Church house! So, I had to be in "something", too! The part they failed to mention in the fine print was, being in "something" meant being in ERRTHANG!! Junior Usher, Kids Choir, Youth Choir, Praise Team, Section Leader, Praise Dance, Junior Aspiring Missionary (J.A.M.), Greeter, help with Nursery, Sunday School Teacher, Announcement lady, Hospitality, Drama, Outreach, Children's Church, Media, Drummer...and this was all before age 16! I did it all and had to do it well cuz we didn't have a choice IF I wanted to or not. Nope! Get in position and catch on! And here's a church announcement to hang your thinking on: if bosses ever need to train their employees on work ethic, tell them to go to Church for six months! I promise you they'll be the best employees on site you've ever had! I know it may seem over the top with the laundry list of departments I was apart of, but when you're around kids that do it too, it's no longer looked at as a to-do list. It's fun to be involved. Imma tell you, I had a blast being in 50 different departments lol It's not so bad being around peers that has parents just like yours! Because there's always someone in the same situation as you, we just do it together! Surprisingly, we didn't see it as work, it's just what you do.

So like I said earlier, I didn't start off as a PK. I was summoned to it lol Let me explain...ok so like yeah I grew up in Church and all that but I still wasn't in the role of a Pastors kid, yet. Oh, but when I turned 17 all that shifted! I remember going to my dads for the weekend and he hit me with the, "So, I'm going to be starting a Church." I'm looking around like, what does that mean?! Who's Church?! Oh, you're going to be helping out a Pastor start THEIR Church? Wow that's nice! Such a helpful Honda. It didn't even cross my mind to think of anything further than that! I just knew he wasn't referring to himself in that manner! But uhh, the facts were...you were about to be a PK, precious! Honestly, I didn't think it was going to be a huge transition because we already do a lot in Church anyway, so I'm thinking it'll be the same routine. Sike, nope not even close! Oh, you'll find out why, just wait on it!

Ok, got the breaking news and letting it marinate, but that wasn't even the kicker. I go to my other house to visit my mom a few months later and I get hit with a, "We're branching off to start our Church." Hold on because what conference call did I miss?! Y'all too?! Like right now?! What is in the water?! I'm over here JUST now taking in my dad becoming a Pastor. That way, when I come home to visit my mom I can just be a regular church member but God told you too?!

I'm just trying to understand why didn't God inform me?! Like everybody getting updates and notifications and I'm getting all these "oh and by the way!" Yet again, because we were so involved in Church, I still didn't think it wouldn't be much of a change from my routine now. Tuh, little did I know...

(A) Nobody told me the first law would be, "the world looks at you!" Everybody, and I mean e-ver-y-body notices you! Another church announcement that needs to be said...celebrities have nothing on PK's. PERIODT. You can quote me on that for sure cuz that'll preach lol Now for me, just imagine THAT..doubled! Half the people in Church I didn't even know, but HAD to talk to because you didn't want to be deemed as the unapproachable, mean Pastors daughter. Trust me, people watch and they will go back and tell your parents. I HAVE hold in my reactions because they look to see if I caught "that". Do you know how hard THAT alone is?! Y'all know I see everything and because people know that, when something goes down, all the pressures on me trying to hold my mule and act like I didn't see a thing! Whew, the lens shall follow me ALL the days of my life, Amen...that's another announcement! People I don't even know, can recite my first, middle, last, date of birth and the first car I drove lol Meanwhile, I'm looking like, "Wait, so where do I know you from?

Cuz I think I must've missed it lol" Do you know how awkward it is being caught off guard by someone that knows your whole family lineage and you know NOTHING about them?! Man it's tough out here lol Oh and please don't dare go outside the church, cuz SOMEBODY gone know you! Now, for me, it's like knocked up 10 notches cuz err-body knows my mom and err-body knows my dad! The first thing I'll hear is, "Scuse me, you Patrice's daughter?" Or "You must be Ricky's daughter. You look just like him" A stranger in my eyes telling me vacant memories about that, all the while I'm still tryna figure out who am I talking to?! Sometimes I just want to respond with a, "No, never heard of 'em!" Thinking maybe that'll decrease the conversation! Even if I tried that, I still think I'd be caught in it lol. There are people in the Church with good intentions and conditioned to like you and your family, but with all that liking means a whole lot of noticing, too. It'll almost become their mission to investigate everything you do. From bad habits, to flirting, to talking during service or Sunday school, to you going over the speed limit, to seeing who your circle of friends look like, to who you're dating…or not, to adding you on ALL your social media pages not liking any posts but casually "mentioning" it to you in person. Yeah, we see your works, beloved Please don't be fooled, we may not say much, but one thing we know… are people!

Ok enough with that, let's talk about what is means to "go" to church in my eyes. Like, what does that even look like? How do I say this in the most literal way to understand...I LIVE THERE!! No, that's not a joke....I'm dead serious! I was at church all thee time cuz it was ALWAYS something going on! From a Leadership Meeting to a Choir rehearsal, she, me AND her was in that thang!!

For your average kid, a week looks like school Monday-Friday, Saturday maybe games of sports you're in or hanging with friends and Sunday is a day to sleep in, maybe finish whatever homework you didn't finish either on Friday, and wind down ready to start your week tomorrow. For a kid that goes to Church, it's basically the same except you might...MIGHT, get up a bit earlier and spend a couple of hours at church on Sunday and maybe pop in a few times a month for Bible Study on Wednesday's. For me as a pastor's kids, I ain't nevuh heard of just that! I was booked to capacity from jump! Let me break down MY week: Monday was praise dance rehearsal, Tuesday was noon day prayer, Bible Band and Youth

Bible study, Wednesday was corporate Bible study, Thursday was choir rehearsal and Pastoral teaching, Friday night was Youth night, Saturday was Sunshine band. Now when it came to Sunday? That's probably thee busiest day of all. Let's break down what a good Sunday looks like for me. You got your tablet ready still, right?! Sunday means having my whole entire fit ready the night before because getting up Sunday morning trying to piece something together could potentially cause us to be late and we had to open the doors of the Church! My parents had a routine like clockwork. Wasn't too much messing up or slacking on a Sunday morning. Everybody who is a body, better be ready by the time they're walking out the door, hear?! Oh, and I literally meant everybody! If you're in the house, you're leaving the house! Getting there early didn't mean just sitting and waiting for others to come. Nope. I became the clean up crew as soon as we step foot in the House. Fully dressed and all, cleaning, vacuuming, restocking toilet paper, picking up trash, yeah we worked. Now it's time for Sunday School. Mind you, we still haven't eaten breakfast yet! I was in charge of getting the Sunday School books and passing them out to everyone. If, and I mean IF there was no one there to teach the class, guess who by default was next in line? YOU ALREADY KNOW! So which means, I had to know the lesson ahead of time for the just in case. Switching roles, we became the Usher to collect the offering in Sunday School.

Sometimes even turning into the Accountant counting the money in the back row. During the 10-15 min break before church starts, now we ate breakfast. A grab and go. Someone always had "donuts in the back", that was the fuel to hold everybody until church was over. Now church starts...but please don't think this is where my break ended. This is where it starts! Everything before church was just a warm up lol At any given time I could be called to do something. If someone was not in place, I became that replacement! I can't tell you how many times I've been called out of my seat to open with praise and worship or be an usher or even play the drums...on the spot. Especially when we're just getting started in Ministry. Listen, I was all things to all men lol After Sunday School, church service and standing around waiting for my parents talk to every single person in the Church, we're the last ones to leave making sure the doors are locked and everything was safe and secured. We'd either eat out, eat Sunday dinner at home or get invited to someone house for dinner. Either way, we ate lol

You'd think that would be the end of it, huh?! Jokes on you! That's just ONE day of one week. This doesn't even include the sidebars of the Revivals that lasted all week, the Midnight musicals, YPWW, Good Friday Service, Sunrise Service, 5am Prayer, Noon Day Prayer, Conferences, Sunshine Band, Easter Programs, Hallelujah Night (Ain't no Halloween, it Hallelujah night...we saved lol), Tarrying Service, Baptism, Youth Congress all week, Vacation Bible School (VBS) in the summer all week, AIM all week, Convocation all week, Shut Ins that started Friday night to Saturday night and back to church Sunday morning for 8am service with an Anniversary Service and 6pm Service. Oh, AND if I didn't do my chores or finish my homework, best believe THAT had to done and done by Sunday night before I went to bed! Im telling y'all, y'all Managers and CEO's better get you a PK on your team! We'll get things done and pray things out! We KNOW what we know cuz we know why we know! Get it?! You'll catch that later lol

Not only that, I learned discipline at a VERY young age! Don't be with friends, and mama or grandma catch you talking in Church. Chiiiiiiile you would've thought your whole life was over! It didn't matter WHERE I was sitting, if she made eye contact with me and give me that "look"...ISSA WRAP!! Y'all know what look I'm talking about lol That look where you better zip it shut real quick, fast and in a hurry! She's for SURE taking me to that bathroom and beating my tail and didn't care WHO seen it!! And I BET NOT be still crying going back in Church cuz she'd take me BACK out and repeat the cycle!!! But my mom didn't play!! She would be in the choir and walk OFF the stage from singing and take my tail to that good bathroom and wish somebody would say something lol Now here's the thing, she would send out warnings, tho. You ever get people or Ushers come up to you like, "Your mom said you talking too much" or "Your mom looking at you?" I'd get it right for a minute thinking she can't see me, oh but let HER take action! She's had it!! Warning comes before destruction and clearly I had been warned! For those who had Grandma or Big Mama around, that wasn't no better lol SHE DID NOT PLAY!! She would have me move NEXT to her...IN THE FRONT ROW if she caught me talking! Lawd talk about embarrassing lol Everyone knew, if I was sitting next to Grandma I had gotten into some kind of trouble. Oh and please believe it was going to be a thorough discussion after Church! Oh yeah, they wanted to know WHY we were talking, what was so important that I needed to share and what did I learn from the message! Ma'am, I don't know! I was with my friends, we seen something hilarious and couldn't stop laughing. The end! Bro, this is real life stuff we dealt with!

For those oblivious to any and everything I've been ranting on about thus far, it would definitely seem like uhhh yeah I'll pass on all of that! But in reality, it was probably some of the best experiences of my life! Yeah, it was a lot but it was a lot with people who you grew to be friends with. Imagine doing the same thing and finding others your age doing the exact same too! It makes it that much easier because you know, where I go, I know a few people going too!

I've met so many people in Church that I still rock with years later! Not just from my primary Church but visiting Churches, concerts, midnight musicals all waiting for our parents to stop fellowshipping!

Y'all still with me?! Oh I can't hear nobody in here!! Y'all not talking back! Ok ok sorry, I'm done!! I'm sure if I give ANYONE reading this, the mic, you could quote a saying that a Pastor has said while preaching! Y'all can't tell me y'all can't! I lowkey want to hear the sayings y'all got tho! So, if you're bold enough, message me some sayings and you just may see them on my social media pages **(IG: @iamdomojones)!!** Don't forget to add your social media names so I can tag you! Now, where were we?!...Ok, you all have seen the commonalities of of being a PK in both denominations, now, let's get to the differences! Whew this is about to be juicy! I mean, well I hope lol It's not really that juicy, maybe that was a stretch but you catch my drift lol Let's just say more interesting rather! Anywho, let's get to it! Y'all just want to know...and I just WANT y'all to know!

It's Personal:

Not everyone knows what it feels like
to be hurt AND anointed.

~ Domo

"*Sunday* Best"

So, let's talk about the dress code one time for the one time, because this is very important in COGIC! This is thee golden rule: don't be coming to the Church house looking like you didn't try...cuz go back home and try again! Let me tell you, we get our clothes out Saturday night and have them hung outside our closet! Jewelry, hat, shoes, stockings (cuz Holiness is still right) and a hat if you feeling sanctified! You can't half do it coming to Church. Men: two or three piece suits off tops! Cuff links, tie, suspenders if you grown grown, socks, watch, handkerchief and flower pin. That's just on casual Youth Sunday! Women: dress or top and bottom, jewelry must be a statement piece. No like foreal, a shine, shimmer, colorful something must be on the earrings, necklace and wrists! Purse must be an eye catcher and shoes?! Please don't play because heels are a must...with some flats or slides in hand! Oh, we're ONLY wearing our shoes when Church starts! Once it's over, better believe you'll be seeing us holding our heels in hand, laughing with you like it's nothing! Church hats are essential for the Muthas of the Church and/or during Official Day and Holy Convocation. I promise you, they're like dawg on masterpieces of head wear lol I've always wanted to walk up to one of the Muthas and ask, "Does your head ever feel like it's leaning from the weight of it?!" Look, I personally can't do it, but every woman I've seen worn a hat has done it well! I may have to find out what stores y'all go to so I can be ready. Cuz if I you stay ready, you ain't got to get...y'all know the rest!

Imma keep it 100 with you, I've never really quite fit in the mold of the Sunday Best category! First of all, I cringe with like all that bling and uncomfort! You not gone have my sliding and sad...it don't match! If you've seen my style, you'd know like too many prints and styles that most people probably wouldn't wear! If everyone is wearing all black, I'm wearing black with highlighter yellow earrings, polka dot glasses, highlighter sneakers, my backpack and black lipstick! THAT'S ME! So you can imagine when I walk in a Church full of Saint John's, three piece suits and shoulder pads, the looks I get! Let me put it from my perspective. I don't dress like this to be rebellious or stubborn, I dress the way I do because I have to think about what's convenient. Having a physical disability, sometimes I can't wear all that because I literally can't put it on. I have a hard time with zippers, buttons, and other sensory things that may be easy for the average, so I dress based on what I can maneuver myself.

Heels don't work for me. Hear me, I will NOT have my ankles any more weak tryna impress you with a dawg on heel! But sneakers do! So you better believe I'm gonna be putting on a dress with these sneakers and watch you walk in with your slides until Church starts! Purses don't work for me. I use a walker so I need something that's hands-free. So you better believe I'm going to be carrying his backpack on my back with his dress on and not think twice about wearing a purse to make me seem like I'm just as girly as the next! I don't have full physical mobility to do my own hair, so I have locs. And you better believe I'm gonna be styling and wrapping these here locs just as much as someone with a press and curl, tuh! So, if I don't get asked to take a picture with you, because my "fit" isn't up to par, it will never be! I've outgrown the par!! And truth be told, if my mom approves of how I represent me, I ain't thinking about any of y'all, in Jesus name!

Let's hop on over to Non-Denom. I know for a fact they've never heard of a Sunday dress code! Never heard of it! They wear what's comfortable and not what's appeasing to the eye. They're not thinking about how they nor how you think they look. They're here and that's that! From sundresses to cargo shorts, jeans to leggings, you're getting it all on Sunday! If "Come as you are" was a person, look at everyone in Non Denom and there you have it!

There's not too much to say about the dress code because they're not doing ALLA that! Slap on something clean, put on lotion and let's roll! We ain't tryna be late!

So listen, for me, this one was an adjustment! Not so much the dress code because I'm going to dress comfortable not for compliments nor compatibility **#MESSAGE**, but because the simple fact that EVERYONE was casual. Like, oh this is actually the protocol and dressing up is outta place! It's like a total flip...and loved it! I fit right on in, finally! I didn't look like I was dressed down for not wearing something with rhinestones or shoulder pads. I had my leggings and high top Jordan's and walked on in with grace, hear?! Not one person even looked twice at me nor stopped me to nonverbally ask me if I knew I was going to Church! Because what does my dress code have to do with what's going on during Service?! Imma be sitting behind you, anyway! If you don't say Amen and turn to YOUR neighbor lol

Here's where it's wack to be in the limelight. We as PK's often hear the saying, "PK's are the worst ones". Now imma defend us right there because A) trust me when I tell you, there are others that top us 2) you magnify what you seek after. People expect us to be thee holiest of them all just because of who our parents are. So, we're automatically stereotyped as one to follow their path as well. SIKE. That ain't us!! Although I'm not considered "worse", I understand why we go that route. Any and everything we do is under a magnifying glass. So, in essence, we could be doing the same thing as someone else's child or someone you know, but because of our parents role, it's looked at as "worse". Ma'am...Sir most of the time we're with YOUR child! Oh, but you didn't look at who was driving tho, got it! If we listen to anything other than "Jesus on the Main Line" or "This is the Day" we're heathens. And let me tell y'all a thing or two about me and my playlist, please DO NOT expect to only hear Gospel, CCM or Christian Rap in my rotation. You'd be very disappointed lol From "Alabaster Box" to "Ice Box" and Imma throw in a few "Shackadelic Shack that's where's its at" then hop on over to a lil Shania Twain...and back to "You Brought The Sunshine." Be prepared to broaden your music registry. If we go anywhere other than Church, Bible Study or a Revival, we're not walking the straight and narrow. If we dance to a song but don't shout in God's House, we going to Hell in a hand basket. And I will do a little shoulder shimmy in a minute...to ANYTHING! If we show too much skin or don't wear stockings to Church we're carnal. If we wear red lipstick...which I have AND wear every color to church on Sunday, we have a Jezebel spirit. And another thing...why ERRTHANG gotta be Jezebel?! We got all these Bible Scholars and Theologians but y'all can't choose another name to use?! . If we miss ONE Bible Study or Sunday service, we must be backsliding or wavering in our walk. A bit extreme huh? Oh, and please don't have a tattoo...which I have 14 and probably setting up an appointment to get another next week, you must be the Captain of satan's whole army! Well, that's the reaching we get...on a daily...from EVERYBODY. You wouldn't imagine the scrutiny I've gotten for walking in Church with pants on and was asked if my mom knew that I was coming to Church like *that?! And if looks could kill, I know for a fact there would be my funeral service in order from all the looks I've gotten from the Saints and Ain'ts when I walk in without stockings and sneakers.* Since when did wearing pants become a crime, nevertheless a sin? I don't think you wanna know my response lol I was respectful tho but I was also an adult then can respectfully respond, Amen lol. I've heard it all. I've been called a trouble maker because of my tats, black lipstick and blue hair. I've been seen as stuck up because people would think I shop at all the high end stores and had all the name brands. Chile, I went on over to the clearance at the Nordstroms Rack and came up! Don't let the style fool you, I don't need a name because I am the brand, tuh! (Get it?! Name? Brand?! Lol) I would always be seen as perfect, never doing anything wrong because of how people sized me up just by my looks...uhh my parents can tell you how off that view is lol I was portrayed as goody too shoes because I didn't drink or smoke and prolly never will. I WAS TOO SICK! My body never was off any medication or out of a surgery long enough to even try it lol AND I had severe asthma, so any smoke made it worse!! Even car smoke lol What I look like using what creates my sickness?! Make it make sense!! That ain't my testimony! What you choose to do, consume or try does not have anything to do with me, beloved! So don't feel bad if I respectfully decline, I want to remember what I did at all times and hear it from someone else lol.

I can't even front, sometimes the avoidance of getting involved in anything, as innocent as it could be, has overpowered my actions because I am constantly watched. In their minds, it seems we're mandated to perfection and purity because of our parents, oh but do I have a huge news flash for you beloved. And hear me clear when I say this: Don't think because our parents are in it, we're taking up their crosses and following there footsteps. Lean in a little bit...I ain't! Nope, nah, I'll pass, no, not even...everything that equivocates to NO, is a hard no for me! And I stand firm on that! And another thang...just because we're PK's does NOT automatically write us off as marrying a Pastor! Aht aht we're not naming nor claiming that, hear?! This ain't no "taking over the family business" or "generation of Pastors" type flow! I'm marrying thee UN-titled, k? A regular church pew member of the Gospel! Maybe someone that works in security watching the cars but that's as far as we're getting! Y'all ain't gone worry me! While I'm over here talking mess, watch me marry the Arch Bishop of the First Jurisdiction of New Baptist Fellowship lol

Before you assume the worst about us, trust me it's not done out of rebellion or to prove a point of how much we're not going to follow in our parents footsteps. That's far from it. The truth is...we see a lot. We have front row seats to the real of everything, how things really flow and who the "saints" really are. As my dad would say, "there's always a scene behind the seen." We don't just see the productions and fluff that's shown on Sundays or Wednesday's. We don't just see the "Ive been praying for you" members that walk up to you at church.

We don't just see the "faithful supporters behind our Pastor" that people show on Sundays. I think the hardest part of it all is seeing my parents at their highest and their lowest...from the stabbing of the saints and the world alike. The ones in the church will cut just as deep as the ones out. Yet, me as a PK, still have to pose as though I know nothing and smile...with love. Wheeeew, let me tell y'all. Me? That's hard. To be truthful, that's probably one of thee harder things about this walk of life. No matter how much parents try to shield us from the worst aspects of church, it is impossible. I've seen my parents get disrespected, threatened, dragged and lied on by people I thought were respectable, without my parents ever exposing anything or anyone about them...still to this day. But the worse part of it is, those same saints and aint's will try to use me to get at my parents and cause a big rift in the church. I told you..we know people. Others may only see the public displays of respect for ministry, but PK's see the ugly moments when the masks come off. What's the life of a PK? You see everything but say nothing. You know a lot but don't speak a thing.

Let me tell y'all, like foreal foreal it's lonely at the top. Not comparing that statement to the rich and famous, being a PK, amongst others your age. Because there are so few peers that can relate to the challenges of ministry, we often feel lonely and isolated. Now PK's probably won't admit that because they want to maintain the "look" but I'll be the first to admit...it's lonely as all get out. It's awkward to show we have feelings. People don't think it's a normal look to say we're dealing with anything because it's simple, "The Pastor is your dad." What problems do you really have? Oh, you think you're going to hell because you didn't pray before you ate? Or you forgot to read your Bible before prayer? It's hard voicing the things we deal with because it's either considered not a real problem or we have to be careful how much we say to avoid exposing family ties to the public or members. I hear the obvious question you ask.."why don't you just go to your parents?" Well here's where our reality hits. Our parents work outside of ministry and do ministry outside of work. There is always someone calling, texting, messaging and walking up to my parents about some thing...all day, no cut off time. Ministry isn't something you can just turn off or punch a time clock and be done with. After your 10 minute call, there was 50 before you and they'll be 50 after you. Not to mention all the mandatory church events, impromptu counseling sessions, and mountains of prayerful study time that mandates preachers away from their families. Let's not forget about the meetings, administrative work, conferences, ministry-related travel, and the business of life in general. And that's just the tip of the iceberg. There's already times where we barely see our parents and if we do, it's either in passing or the next day.

I've literally gone days without seeing my parents. Either they're gone early to work and by the time they get home from something at the church or a ministry event, I'm sleep. Then the cycle repeats. And after all that from the outside, then be expected to add one more person on the inside too? Just cause I feel like I need to talk? Let me ask you, would you? Didn't think so. So what do we do? Suffer in silence. Just deal with it. We learn how to cope to the best of our ability. We participate. We lead services and activities that others don't want to be bothered with. We welcome people into our home—no matter what. We welcome people into our home...no matter what. We welcome people into our home...NO MATTER WHAT! Cuz walking out of my room to find a meeting happening in the dining room or living area isn't weird anymore! It's just another Tuesday lol We get to the church early and leave late, and we learn to keep our family business in our house—especially your own. My mindset goes to even say, it won't be understood because they can't relate anyway. Ashamed to voice my opinion to fit in? Oh yeah that's definitely apart of a PK's hidden thoughts. You still think PK's don't deal with anything?

Let's start here...service times! Now look this one took me out!! If you grew up COGIC, then you know service is a MINIMUM of six to seven hour days on Sundays! That's the bare minimum! Now, there's two different types of Church services: The church with one service which is typically the rather smaller churches or the church with three to four services, which is how the Mega Churches run their services. Either way...you were in that thang like you clocked in for work!

What does that look like Dōmo? I'm glad you asked! So we just gone talk about me, mmmkay?! A typical Sunday growing up was 8am Service, then Sunday School, then go to the choir room to get a danish or donuts for breakfast or go to the liquor store with the crew and buy something to hold you cuz you ain't leaving no time soon! 9:45 Service was next. Either you'd go to Children's Church or Youth Church. But depending on the day, sometimes your mom would just make you stay in church and sit up close. There was never a particular reason other than "...because I said so!".

And that was that! After 9:45 service, we either went out to dinner, came home to change or just stayed at the church and took a nap in the back overflow because we had to be right back at church for 6 pm service. We'd typically be heading home around 8:30/9 which SOLELY depended on how much talking my parents would do after church, then walking to the car, then at the car, then getting in the car AND driving off the parking lot! Oh yeah, there's levels to this lol. That was a typical Sunday morning growing up COGIC.

Now, I said I was brought up in two different denominations right?! Being raised COGIC, now switching under Nondenominational practices at age 22, here's where the pivot officially begins! Whew, alright so boom. When I started Nondenominational, prayer started at 9:30, church started at 10 am and we were walking to our cars by 12:30pm...wait...and that's including fellowshipping with saints after church! I said wait...where's the rest?! Ain't no part two?! No extended version?! That's it?! Oh wait, there's more! WHATS A NIGHT SERVICE?! Come back, when?! Not Sunday night, tuh! I mean done done!! Listeeeeen, y'all like real talk, I didn't know what to do with myself the first time I went to Nondenom! I was like uhhh I can't just GO home and have the rest of my day, like naw! There has to be more!! I'm so used to doing at least three services on Sundays,

I felt like I didn't go to church at all being done by 12! I was foreal lost for a while trying to find a church to attend to make up them extra five hours of new free time I was given lol Oh but a wonderful change, huh?!!!

It's Personal:

I have to realize I'm always on an interview with God...i should always be updating my resume on a daily.

~ Domo

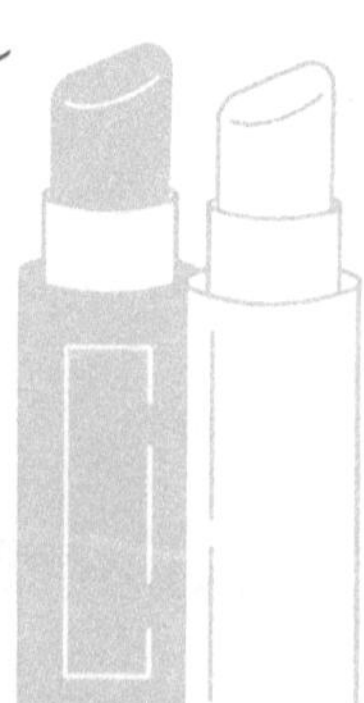

"We Don't Need No Music, All We Need Is The Holy Ghost"

Now listen! In COGIC, if the music ain't right, you may wanna rethink what you're there for lol From the songs to the choir director to the lead to the band...EVERYTHING IS ESSENTIAL! A choir song? Check. A dope drummer? Needed. Click track? Of course. A lead singer that has range? Essential. An energetic choir director? They're in position. Tambourine? I brought one in with me. You catch my drift! Don't come to a service and expect anything less than a whole concert when the choir sings. That's normal lol Songs like "I wish somebody soul would" and "I don't know what you've come to do" were songs that ERRBODY knew...by default. If you grew up COGIC, it's two things you will learn: you knew how to shout and you knew all the toe tappers. Ain't nothing like the entire church, from young to old, singing the same song! And don't let someone bring a tambourine in there! It's a wrap, bro. Tambourines pretty much had their own section lol There would literally be a group of people in one section with their tambourines ready, willing and able for that track to hit. "We don't need no music (dun dun), all we need is the Holyghost."

And we can't forget about when someone you don't even know, turns around to give you that "let me play" look! It's the best feeling because you were getting tired and you don't really want to stop playing when it gets good but they came in the knick of time, and so you toss them the tambourine and once they catch it, they go IN like it's nobody's business! The way you start rooting them on like a cheerleader is that serious because you're just so proud they matched your energy. Now we've become tambourine buddies for life and from now on every time we see each other, it's a whole tambourine tag team at every church function for life! Let me just say, this story is me! I am her and she is me! Yeah, I was one of those "let me play" tambourine buddies lol Real talk, I've met a lot of friends who I'm still friends with today from a tambourine! Soooo as Missionary Eve said, "Get your tambourine, gone and get yourself a whistleblower!"

Let's get to the Non-Denom. Uhhhh it's simple…they don't do all that! Shouting?! Ehhh too fast and too much extra noise, it don't take all that ruckus lol And truth be told, most of music played is of a slower ballot, so even if you try to hit that track, they gone be looking at you like, "What am I supposed to be doing with this?!" For the COGIC folk to understand, they clap on the 1 & 3! Need I say more?! Naw but in all honesty, what I've learned mostly about attending a Non-Denom, they are pure worshippers.

They don't need much and it don't take much. They will "stay right there" for as ever long as it takes. Forget programs, protocols and preaching, if God is moving, all bets are off and they're going to let Him do Him. Every single time. It's the pure essence for me! I know for a fact, since becoming Non Demon, my worship is at a whole different level like foreal! Three words repetitively is enough for me lol I don't even know if I like a click tracks as much anymore because it's too loud lol Can we just sing like a big choir and stay right there?! I can't be doing all that moving and gliding anyway, my legs ain't legging like they used to! Give them a good simple chorus that everyone can sing along too and thassit boss. On the flip side, they groove! What does that mean Domo?! Don't expect a "rocking side to side" type feel. FORGET ABOUT IT!! Imma include me on this one because if anyone has seen me at church during Praise & Worship, then you KNOW how I gets down in my corner! Shoulders in full action lol Two stepping...with my walker cuz we are not tryna fall, Amen lol...something mean, ok?! We don't play when it comes to nice little groove now. WE WILL DANCE!! And if it gets real good, we'll find someone that's singing in the choir on stage, make eye contact and start grooving together lol BUT WAIT THERE'S MORE!! If it gets gooder than good, the Praise Team leader will turn the whole congregation into a dance shuffle! We WILL lean with it, rock with it, with a quickness! I'm just saying!

Now, shall we get into tithes and offering tho?! I think so!! Let's go with Non-Denom first. Ok sooooo yeah, uhhh, they took the scripture "Each one must give as he has decided in his heart, not grudgingly or necessity, for God loves a cheerful giver" literal cuz we don't even TALK about giving! Yes, we bring it up because it is important but it's real light weight, though. I feel like it's an honorable mention lol We give either online or on the way out the door and put your monetary donation in a black box as you're leaving so no nosies can see what's being given! Cuz you know they do lol Matter of fact, we don't even call it offering, it's a contribution or donation to the Ministry! Recently, we changed it to where we all walk around for offering, but that's only sometimes if the Spirit ain't moved that Sunday, but the offering box is still black! Can't nobody see what you're giving shoot! So Imma speak for me, offering is when I get my "hi's" and "hey gurl", hugs and laughs in cuz uhhh I ain't taking a lap round that whole church! My legs would be done for and typically everyone has to pass by me anyway, so what better way to get all my acknowledgments just in case

I don't see them after service! Hey, it makes sense to me! That's wisdom, tuh!

COGIC? Total opposite, my friend! I know for a fact, offering was pretty much another Church service! We spent at good 30-45 minutes to do offering! Let me break it down for y'all! We did the first half of service, then it's "offering time" where everyone has to stand up and hold up your envelope while one of the Elders pray for the offering. The choir stand is first to bring their offering down to the front and shimmy right on the back up to the stand to sing an offering song. Then the Ushers go row by row escorting us to walk to the front, drop off our offering, and walk back to our seats. We really used that time as our own Runway to show off our Sunday Best outfits...but y'all didn't hear that from me lol Oh and we ALL had to get up and walk around for offering. If you didn't have anything to give that day? Either tap the receptacle or get some lint out your pocket and place it in the offering by faith, but you walking around, tuh! After everyone walks around and the Deacons gather the offering to put it in one tray, one of the Elders get back up to the mic and pray again to seal everyone's giving and we finish the order of service. And that's on a regular Sunday...And to whom it may concern, just to throw this out there since I have the mic: MONEY LINES ARE NOT IN THE BIBLE! I sure did say it with boldness! As you were...

There are also days where there needs to be a certain budget met and they would have a $1,000, $500, $100, $50, $25, "find someone to go half with" and "whatever you have to give" money lines to meet those needs. The Pastor or Deacon would set out a mandate of declaration that we can't "move along with the service" until we reach our goal. Hence the money lines begin. If when it's counted, we're still short, wherever we are in the service would immediately come to a haul to to make another announcement of the balance we still have left to meet. Let me tell y'all, WE AREN'T MOVING ALONG IN SERVICE TILL IT'S MET, hear?! Trust and believe them musician will gladly play some elevator music while we wait! At this point is where the "find someone to go half with" and "whatever you have to give" comes into play. Money lines ain't working, just COME! They don't care where you come from! They just tryna meet this goal and pay these people! Been on this same goal for an hour! Tap your neighbor and say, "Pop your collar just give a dollar!"

As many offerings as I've witnessed and even joined in, I've just never understood the money lines! That was literally my intermission to go outside, talk to my friends foreal without getting in trouble or take a bathroom break. . I knew I had a good 45 minutes to spare, so we gone make the best of it. And I was tired anyway?!

Listen, I gotta keep my energy up before you see me knocked out in this back row! I always thought, and MAYBE it's just me...if we didn't have the money to support the event, and we have to beg and plead the Saints for it, shouldn't it just have not even been a thing? I mean, if we gone stick with the Bible, Iont know everything but I DO know it states, "Wages, like a debt owed, MUST BE PAID". Now riddle me this, if we ain't paid them because we're banking on the money lines to, why can't we just say not this time boss. It ain't in the budget?! But who am I?!

Prayer is essential on both ends. Let me make that very clear! Oh, WE GONE PRAY! Now, the difference is the "How"! Let's get into it, shall we?! Non-Denom? Let's just say, they get straight to it! They don't need too much of an introduction to it all, just saying exactly what we're praying about and that's a wrap. It doesn't take much to get to the point lol The conversation is very minimal and easy to the point where anyone can be apart of. It's almost like you're chilling with the homies and you overhear two of your friends having a real deep conversation. Although you don't say anything, you still walk over and and be apart because you can relate. It's like that! It makes you want to get in on the conversation because you get everything that's being said. Non Denom prayers is talking to the Big homie! There, I said it! Although you know exactly how much authority the Big homie has, He's so down to earth and relatable, it's not hard talking to Him. He's the Savior, but He's also my guy lol You get it?! (The way I described it is hilarious to my own self lol)

So here's the thing, when I first heard one of

the members at our Church pray, "God, you already know what I'm about to say but Imma still tell you. I've been staying saved but if I keep getting tested. Your people are going to take me back and I may just let them if You don't step in on my behalf." I said woah, woah, woah wait huh?! Am I overhearing your conversation with your friend or is this how you pray on a daily?! The fact that I was the only one that opened my eyes in confusion, while everyone was in agreement, was wild! Oh, so this the norm?! Ok well let's a get it! The freedom to pray your way, was the best eye opener I've ever experienced. It made me want to just talk to God like I talk to Him. Fun fact: HE ALREADY KNOWS US! Why not talk to him like we know that?! Ain't no sugarcoating nor fluffy verbiage during prayer! With reverence, we say it with our chest!

Bowed Heads. The Master of them All..We Thank You! Thee Author and Finisher of our faith, we come boldly before the Throne of Grace! Can. You. See. The. Difference?! I mean just prestige, ain't it?! COGIC will come up with sayings that just sound Holy! When it's time to pray, don't think we're sitting down anytime soon because we gotta go through ALL the names of God, nicknames and prefixes too. And that's just the intro! We haven't even touched on what exactly we're praying for! That'll be another 13 minutes to cover!

"And we'll be so careful to give your Name all the glory that is due You." I still don't know why we have to be careful?! But here's the grand finale..."...in your matchless Name." Your what?! What is matchless?! I mean, I'm sure it means no one can even compare to...but I meeeeeeean these words are so profound! Now, I will say, there has been a plethora of times when it gets real good and you have to just enter in! Especially when you know who's praying, been warring in their prayer closet?! Listen, ain't nothing like it! You can literally feel the presence of God on your shoulders (I just quickened!). And don't let someone speak in tongues AND interpret it?! You might as well just pick me up from the floor because I'm slain! Or I have one better, get you a good Church Mother to pray!! Myyyyy God tuhday! All they have to say is "Jesus, Jesus, Jesus!" That's it! THAT'S THE PRAYER! That's a whole entire tarrying service right there!

On the other hand, There's the times I ask myself, "What the what?!" Who sent you?! I mean just all over the place and confusing! I didn't pick up not a thing you threw down, Deacon! I can't keep up! I can't overlook the fact that it definitely shows a form of reverence to our King showing who He is, but uhhh is there a condensed version?! A cheat sheet, even?! Asking for a friend! (I'm the friend lol) And Lawd, don't let the beloved be long winded!

That's where I draw the line! At this point, I feel like sometimes people need bullet points to stay on track! They get the mic and get a little too excited! I know we're supposed to have our eyes closed, but thank God for grace and understanding! Read that cheat sheet! I'm real quick to sit my little happy self down and tend to my business while you get it out your system! I definitely have gotten a lot few look's because I've sat down during prayer while everyone else has another 26 minutes to go, but my legs are not having that! Your eyes should be closed anyway, you're distracted lol Keep your focus on this long winded prayer lol

It's Personal:

If you love yourself,
it won't be as hard loving people.

~ Domo

After the tally's are counted and the differences are addressed, one message stays the same. Jesus. That's the foundation of everything we do. From one blood He made ALL the Nations...including Denominations! Shed the layers of religion, rituals and relatability, we all just tryna make it to Heaven! Growing up from opposite traditions, just gave me a better perspective that there's more than one way to please God. He's no respect of person, SO if you decide to wear heels and a brooch or slides and shorts, if y'all both are lifting up the name of Jesus, what else is there to discuss?! Goal accomplished! Keep doing you boo, and do it well! Moving right along...

Ok so Domo, peró like, but what's life like being a PK (y'all should know the term by now lol)?! Listeeeeeen, let me break it all the way down for you. You ready? Ok so boom...DON'T TRY TO KEEP UP WITH THE JONESES! And I am a Jones lol There's definitely a standard holding the position of a PK. Especially when it's just a fold you were put in because you're the seed of your parents.

Nevertheless, trying to perfect what a PK should look like. Be like. Sound like or say, is a standard that's nonexistent. I'm me. Before the title and after the title. I have tattoos, piercings, a walker that colorfully decorated every few months, blue hair (...this month lol) and wear sneakers to Church every Sunday and I wish someone would try to say something contrary to what MY Bible calls me! I'm a heathen to some but I'm a servant to His people and everyone knows who I represent. I call Him Lord over my life. No questions asked. I don't need no special greeting or no reserved seat. Well, maybe just one off to the side so I'll have some space for my walker to park, but the point is...you get it shoot!

Sooooo yeah, that's my story and I'm sticking to it! I mean look at you, making it to the whole end and such! You a real one and you're alright with me! Well y'all, the hour is drawn nye and I'm about to go get some fruit snacks and most likely start getting ready for SOMETHING we're having at Church lol **#LifeOfAPK** If you see me on the street, make sure you say "Heeeeey, Domo!" LOVE YOU, ALWAYS Oh last thing before you close the book. Raise your right hand and repeat after me, "When I say unto One, I say unto all. Watch. And Pray!" Lol ok foreal, bye!